D0371421

THE
ARTISANAL
KITCHEN

SWEETS
& TREATS

THE
ARTISANAL
KITCHEN

SWEETS
& TREATS

33 CUPCAKES, BROWNIES, BARS, *and* CANDIES
to MAKE *the* SEASON EVEN SWEETER

CHERYL DAY AND GRIFFITH DAY

ARTISAN | NEW YORK

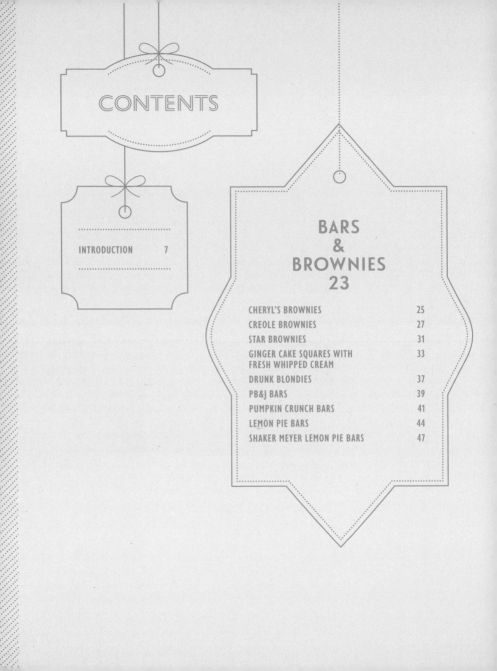

CONTENTS

CUPCAKES
51

CANDIES
77

INTRODUCTION

Many people's kitchens turn into a veritable baking wonderland when the holiday season sets in, and there is nothing quite like the satisfaction of bringing smiles to the faces of those enjoying your delicious creations. The process of baking intimidates many folks, but our style of baking is meant to be fun. Once you master a few simple techniques, you're in! It's the small details that make all the difference. Becoming a great baker is accessible to anyone who is willing to learn. Here are our simple but special tricks for turning out incredible snacks and baked goods.

READ THE RECIPE

Always read a recipe from start to finish to make sure that you have a clear understanding of all the steps. It's a mistake to assume that, for example, because you have made cupcakes many times you know the method for every single cupcake recipe. Think of a recipe as your baking GPS. Be sure that you have the proper tools and that all of your ingredients are at the proper temperature. One of the most common kitchen errors is to start mixing and then discover that you are missing a key ingredient. Yikes!

Another common mistake is to not realize that an ingredient—say, sugar—is added in two separate increments, not all at once. If you don't read the instructions, you are not setting yourself up for success. So say it with me: "Read the whole recipe first!"

ORGANIZE YOUR WORKSPACE (AND YOUR MIND)

Your most important tool in baking is a clean and organized workspace. Make sure that you have all of your ingredients and tools prepped and ready to go before you start baking. The French term *mise en place* means, literally, to "put in place." Measure out the flour and sugar, chop the nuts, and have clean bowls ready. Many baking techniques are time-sensitive—it is disastrous to start mixing only to realize that you needed to get your butter or eggs to room temperature first. Distractions are often the villains in the kitchen: if you have to stop for a phone call, be sure to make a note of where you left off in the recipe so that you don't find yourself trying to recall whether you added the salt or not. A well-organized kitchen will ensure confidence and success.

TEMPERATURE MATTERS

It is essential to have your ingredients at the temperature called for in the recipe. For example, if your eggs are too cold when you add them to your perfectly creamed butter and sugar, the butter will seize up, deflating the air bubbles that you worked so hard to create, and the batter will resist being completely mixed. If that happens, the air bubbles will not expand during baking and the result will be a flat, dense cupcake, not one with a light, fluffy, and tender crumb.

The quickest way to get eggs to room temperature is simply to put the whole eggs in a small bowl of hot water and swish them around for 1 to 2 minutes, being careful not to bang their delicate shells against one another. This will bring them gently to room temperature. Don't leave them in the hot water too long, though, or you will begin to cook them.

If a recipe calls for room-temperature butter, that means it is between 65° and 67°F, which is cool but not cold. You can pull the butter out of the refrigerator about an hour before you are going to start (on a superhot day, 30 minutes will do the trick), or you can cut it into cubes to help speed up the process of bringing it to room temperature. A few visual and tactile clues can also help you to determine whether or not butter is at the proper temperature: you should be able to make an indentation with your finger on the surface of the butter, but the butter should be slightly firm, not hard—and definitely not squishy. If the butter gets too warm, label it with the date and return it to the refrigerator for future use for something that does not require creaming. Start again with fresh butter.

PREHEAT YOUR OVEN

Start preheating your oven at least 20 minutes before baking to make sure that it has a chance to come to the correct temperature. You should also use an oven thermometer to make sure your oven is calibrated correctly (see "The Baker's Dozen," page 16). All ovens are not created equal, and baking temperature can make a big difference in the result. If the oven is too cold when you put a cupcake in it, rising will be inhibited, the batter will melt, and the crumb will be tough. If the oven is too hot, the results can be even more disastrous. A crust will form on the outside of cupcake layers and the inside will be underbaked and gooey.

Ovens will cycle on and off during baking, and every time you open the oven door, the temperature will drop slightly. This is why baking times are usually given as a range. If a recipe says to bake for 20 to 25 minutes, check it at the earliest time. And don't worry if your oven takes 5 minutes longer than suggested. Use the visual clues for doneness given with the recipes as well, and always take note of your baking time, which will be helpful the next time you make that recipe.

KNOW YOUR INGREDIENTS

It is important to understand the role of each ingredient in the baking process. You can't just skip over steps or substitute ingredients and think it will all work out in the end.

Take the unassuming egg: it performs so many important functions in making baked goods and other desserts. Eggs leaven, thicken, moisturize, and enhance flavors. Whole eggs, as well as yolks on their own, are great emulsifiers. The lecithin in yolks binds fats and water, which normally resist each other. Eggs also provide structure; when egg whites are whipped to stiff peaks and folded into a batter, for example, the air trapped in the whites expands in the heat of the oven during baking, acting as a leavening agent for light, airy desserts.

Baking soda and baking powder are both leaveners. They create chemical reactions in doughs and batters that release carbon dioxide bubbles that will cause cake layers to rise. Baking soda requires the presence of an acid, such as sour cream, buttermilk, molasses, nonalkalized cocoa powder, or brown sugar (which contains molasses) to activate it. Baking powder does not require the presence of acid; it reacts once it is combined with a liquid, such as milk. Baking powders made with aluminum compounds have a chemical aftertaste, so we use aluminum-free baking powder in all of our recipes.

TO WEIGH OR NOT TO WEIGH— THAT IS THE QUESTION

Baking is a precise science. At the bakery, we measure out pounds and pounds of flour, sugar, butter, and eggs, and using a scale makes for quick work with large amounts and our busy production schedule. However, as self-taught scratch bakers, we use measuring cups at home and when baking in small batches at the bakery. We know that most home bakers don't own a scale.

Although we realize the importance of accurate measuring, we know this can be achieved with measuring cups as well. We give instructions for measuring certain ingredients properly so that you will achieve consistent results every time you use one of our recipes.

And use the correct vessel to measure: dry measures for dry ingredients, liquid measures for liquids (see "The Baker's Dozen," page 16).

MEASURING DRY INGREDIENTS

When you measure flour or sugar, use this no-fail technique (we recommend storing flour, sugar, and other dry ingredients in a canister rather than a sack so that you have plenty of space to dip and scoop): First loosen up or fluff the flour a bit with your measuring cup or a spoon. Scoop the flour or sugar into your measuring cup until it is heaping, then sweep a straight edge, such as the back of a table knife, across the top to level it. Do not tap the cup to settle the contents (brown sugar, though, is usually packed into the cup).

CREAMING BUTTER

To produce the perfect texture in baked goods, you must master the art of creaming butter, which is the foundation of many recipes. Often recipes start with the words "cream the butter and sugar together," without any explanation of what this actually means. And they fail to tell you that if you don't do this step properly, the results can be disastrous. If your butter is too cold, it will not whip properly; if it is too soft, it will not retain air. The most important factor in creaming butter and sugar is the temperature of the butter. See "Temperature Matters," page 8.

When a recipe calls for creaming butter and sugar, you want to beat the softened butter and the sugar together until the mixture is light in both color and texture; this means air has been incorporated. We've included timing estimates in all the recipes to give you a sense of how long this step will take. Use these estimates as guidelines, but it is also important to learn what the result should look like. Properly creamed butter and sugar will be very pale yellow (or very light brown if you're using brown sugar) and almost doubled in volume.

Remember that baking is a science. The creaming process aerates the butter; air bubbles are literally forced into the butter mixture. These air bubbles expand during baking, giving your baked goods the texture that you want. Once you master this technique, you will be amazed at what a difference it makes. Your cupcakes will have a light, delicate crumb and your cookies will be melt-in-your-mouth delicious.

PRACTICE MAKES PERFECT

My mother always used to say this, and it is certainly true when it comes to baking; even if you mess up every now and then, it's okay. Mistakes may not always be pretty, but they often taste delicious. Whenever you learn a new craft, there will be a learning curve. Take notes and learn from your mistakes. Have fun, and keep smiling along the way, and I promise you will get better every time.

There are many variables to be aware of in baking, but don't let that scare you. One of the things I love most about baking, for example, is the challenge of having to figure things out day after day based on the weather. If it's a hot and humid Savannah day, I know I will have to play some tricks to get my meringues to have perfect peaks. And if it's a really hot day, I may decide not to make chocolates at all and opt for ice cream sammies instead. The more you bake, the more you will learn.

THE BAKER'S DOZEN

There are certain tools for scratch baking that any baker should have in the kitchen. If we were stranded on a desert island (with a kitchen, of course!), these are the twelve tools we would have with us.

1. STAND OR HANDHELD MIXER. Our mothers and grandmothers used a handheld mixer for baking; I remember it was a big deal when my mother bought her first stand mixer, a shiny turquoise Hamilton Beach model with all the attachments. It was like my mom had won the lottery, and I benefited from all the yummy treats she made with it.

You can use a handheld mixer for most of these recipes, but a stand mixer is one of the best investments you'll make if you're a serious baker. A good stand mixer will allow you to cream butter, whip egg whites, make bread and cookie doughs, and mix delicate cake batters. It will give better volume and consistency to your batters and doughs and make easy work out of long mix times. Our recipes use the paddle attachment and the whisk, but our new favorite accessory is an all-in-one paddle attachment with a spatula blade. It scrapes the sides of the bowl as it mixes, saving you from having to do it.

2. MEASURING CUPS AND SPOONS. Measuring cups and spoons are among those tools so familiar that you never stop to think about how important they are. Before measuring spoons, grandma's handwritten recipe would tell you to use a pinch of this and a dash of that to make her lemon pound cake extra special. We can credit Fannie Farmer, the author of *The Boston Cooking-School Cook Book*, for inventing measuring cups in 1896. She helped standardize the measuring of ingredients.

Measuring cups fall into two categories: dry and liquid. Dry measuring cups are for flour, sugar, and other such ingredients. Liquid measuring cups are for any liquid. We suggest you have a few sizes of liquid measures: 1 cup, 2 cup, and 4 cup.

Measuring spoons are used to measure small amounts of both dry and wet ingredients. They usually come in a complete set. The most common measurement sizes are ⅛, ¼, ½, and 1 teaspoon and 1 tablespoon.

3. BALLOON WHISK. Balloon whisks are used to stir batters, whip meringues and cream, and blend custards. The open design of a balloon whisk makes it handy for mixing and aerating dry ingredients if you don't have a sifter — in fact, sifting is easier with a whisk. Whisks come in many different sizes; having a few will enable you to do many different tasks in the kitchen.

4. RUBBER SPATULA, PLASTIC DOUGH SCRAPER, AND METAL BENCH SCRAPER. A rubber spatula is your best tool to get every bit of cupcake batter into the pan (leaving just a little bit behind in the bowl to lick). It also folds beaten egg whites into a batter. A plastic bowl scraper can be used, of course, to scrape out bowls, but we use it to scoop the measured dry ingredients into the mixing bowl. A metal bench scraper is best for dividing bread doughs and for scraping your work surface clean.

5. KNIVES: PARING, CHEF'S, AND SERRATED BREAD. Invest in good-quality knives, along with a steel and a sharpener to maintain them. A paring knife, 3 to 4 inches long, is best for peeling and slicing fruits and other ingredients. A chef's knife that is 6 to 8 inches in length is a utility knife, best for chopping nuts and dried fruit, among other tasks. A serrated bread knife, 8 to 9 inches long, is great for chopping blocks of chocolate, cutting cakes into layers, and, of course, slicing bread.

6. MIXING BOWLS. Mixing bowls come in different sizes and materials, including glass, ceramic, plastic, and stainless steel. We prefer wide heavy-duty stainless steel bowls that make mixing easy. Stainless steel bowls are nonreactive and very durable; a set of six nested bowls from small to large will cover most baking needs. Use glass mixing bowls for melting chocolate and for anything else you want to pop in the microwave to warm.

7. BAKING SHEETS. The debate about the merits of nonstick, dark, and insulated pans seems endless, but paired with nonstick spray or parchment paper, good heavy-duty baking sheets will outperform all others and will last your lifetime. All you really need are two 12-by-17-inch heavy-duty rimmed aluminum baking sheets and one 10-by-15-inch rimmed jelly-roll pan. We speak from experience on this; trust us. You can find these baking sheets, also called sheet pans, at your local restaurant supply store or online.

8. BAKING PANS. For your sweet treats, you want good-quality, sturdy aluminum pans that provide even heat. Avoid thin, lightweight pans that will allow your baked goods to burn.

9. SIFTER. A sifter is a great tool for mixing and aerating dry ingredients; it will also help break up clumps of ingredients. We specify a sifter (or a fine-mesh sieve) for some of the recipes in this book; at other times, using a whisk to aerate the dry ingredients is enough.

10. ROLLING PIN. A simple straight, non-tapered, hand-turned wooden rolling pin is an all-purpose tool. At 16 inches, it is the perfect size and weight for rolling out biscuits and cookies, doughs and piecrusts. I do not recommend marble rolling pins because flour does not stay on them if you dust them before rolling, and they tend to drag and stick on the dough. Take good care of your wooden pin, and it will last for generations, becoming a treasured family heirloom.

11. PARCHMENT PAPER. I can't say enough about the wonders of parchment paper. It's perfect for lining both cookie sheets and brownie pans. It's the best way to create a nonstick surface if you don't want to use a nonstick spray.

12. OVEN THERMOMETER. Whenever someone calls us with a baking problem, we always ask, "Do you have an oven thermometer?" All ovens are not the same, and it's important to know where your oven stands when it comes to maintaining temperature. A properly calibrated oven (even a new oven may be off) is essential for cooking and baking. To test your oven, put an oven thermometer in it, turn it to 350°F, and then check to make sure the oven reaches the proper temperature. If the temperature doesn't read true, adjust the oven temperature until the thermometer reads correctly—and then call a professional to calibrate the oven.

ADDITIONAL TOOLS

Once you've got the basics covered, here are the other tools we recommend.

BOWLS

3-piece glass set: 1-, 1½-,
  and 2½-quart

3-piece stainless steel set:
  1½-, 3-, and 5-quart

POTS, PANS, AND BAKING PANS

6- to 8-quart heavy-bottomed
  nonreactive stockpot
2- to 3-quart heavy-bottomed
  nonreactive saucepan
9-by-13-inch baking pan
9-inch square baking pan

8-inch square baking pan
Two 12-cup muffin pans
Two or more 12-by-17-inch
  rimmed baking sheets
10-by-15-inch rimmed
  jelly-roll pan

UTENSILS AND OTHER TOOLS

Candy thermometer
Fine-mesh duster/sugar shaker
Heat-resistant silicone spatulas
Heat-resistant spoons
Ice cream scoops—small
  (39 mm/1½ tablespoons) and
  large (52 mm/3 tablespoons)
Instant-read thermometer
Kitchen blowtorch
Kitchen scale

Kitchen shears
Offset metal spatulas: small,
  medium, and large
Oven mitts
Pastry bags and tips
Pastry cutter/blender
Plastic dough scraper
Silicone baking mats (Silpats)
Silicone-bristle pastry brush
Stainless steel bench scraper

Straight spatulas: small, medium, and large

Timer

Wire cooling racks

Wire whisks

A WELL-STOCKED SPICE RACK

Every baker should have a range of spices. It's the easiest way to add flavor to your recipes, and you can play with combinations to make recipes unique to you. Keep spices in a cool, dark cupboard and date each bottle when you purchase it. Most spices will lose their potency and flavor after a while. Ground spices will keep for up to 1 year; whole spices will last for several years.

Allspice

Cardamom

Cinnamon (ground and sticks)

Cloves (ground)

Cream of tartar

Fine sea salt (see Tip)

Flaky sea salt, such as Jacobsen or Maldon

Ginger (ground)

Mace

Nutmeg (ground and whole)

TIP: At the bakery, we use only fine sea salt (*sel de mer*) and fleur de sel, a more coarsely ground finishing salt from France. We like the good flavor they add to both sweet and savory dishes. However, you can substitute table salt in any of the recipes that call for fine sea salt, using the same measurement.

BARS &
BROWNIES

CHERYL'S BROWNIES

This brownie is loaded with the good stuff: pure chocolate, crunchy walnuts, and espresso—need I say more? Some brownie purists say there shouldn't be any baking powder in a brownie, but we use a little bit to give it some lift. This is a moist, cakey brownie.

½ CUP UNBLEACHED
ALL-PURPOSE FLOUR

1½ TEASPOONS BAKING POWDER,
PREFERABLY ALUMINUM-FREE

1½ CUPS SEMISWEET
CHOCOLATE CHIPS

6 OUNCES UNSWEETENED
CHOCOLATE, COARSELY CHOPPED

½ POUND (2 STICKS) UNSALTED
BUTTER, CUT INTO CUBES

3 EXTRA-LARGE EGGS

1½ TEASPOONS ESPRESSO POWDER

1 TABLESPOON PURE
VANILLA EXTRACT

1¼ CUPS SUGAR

1 CUP CHOPPED WALNUTS

Position a rack in the middle of the oven and preheat the oven to 350°F. Lightly grease a 9-by-13-inch baking pan and line with parchment, allowing the ends of the paper to hang over two opposite edges of the pan.

In a small bowl, whisk the flour and baking powder together; set aside.

Put 1 cup of the chocolate chips, the unsweetened chocolate, and the butter in a large heatproof bowl, set it over a pot of barely simmering water (do not let the bottom of the bowl touch the water), and stir frequently until the chocolate and butter are melted and smooth. Remove from the heat.

continued

Meanwhile, in a medium bowl, whisk the eggs, espresso powder, vanilla, and sugar together until thoroughly combined.

Add the egg mixture to the chocolate mixture and stir with a wooden spoon until the mixture thickens, 3 to 5 minutes. Sprinkle the flour mixture over the chocolate and mix it until combined. Stir in the walnuts and the remaining semisweet chocolate chips, mixing until just combined.

Pour the batter into the prepared pan and smooth the top with a spatula. Tap the pan firmly on the counter to remove any air bubbles from the batter. Bake for 25 to 30 minutes. Let the brownies cool completely on a wire rack.

Cut the brownies into squares and enjoy. They will keep in an airtight container at room temperature for up to 3 days.

CREOLE BROWNIES

For the people who fall into the "fudgy" camp when it comes to brownie devotion, this one leads that category with a serious ganache topping infused with chicory coffee. The cocoa nibs give the brownie a crunchy yet tender texture.

FOR THE BROWNIES

½ POUND (2 STICKS) UNSALTED BUTTER, CUT INTO CUBES

8 OUNCES UNSWEETENED CHOCOLATE, COARSELY CHOPPED

2½ CUPS SUGAR

½ TEASPOON FINE SEA SALT

2 TEASPOONS PURE VANILLA EXTRACT

4 LARGE EGGS

1 CUP UNBLEACHED ALL-PURPOSE FLOUR

¼ CUP COCOA NIBS (SEE TIP)

FOR THE GANACHE

1 CUP HEAVY CREAM

8 TABLESPOONS (1 STICK) UNSALTED BUTTER, CUT INTO CUBES

⅓ CUP SUGAR

¼ TEASPOON FINE SEA SALT

16 OUNCES BITTERSWEET CHOCOLATE, FINELY CHOPPED

¼ CUP HOT FRESHLY BREWED NEW ORLEANS–STYLE CHICORY COFFEE OR STRONG REGULAR COFFEE

1 TEASPOON PURE VANILLA EXTRACT

FLEUR DE SEL FOR SPRINKLING (OPTIONAL)

Position a rack in the middle of the oven and preheat the oven to 350°F. Lightly grease a 9-by-13-inch baking pan and line with parchment, allowing the ends of the paper to hang over two opposite edges of the pan.

To make the brownies: Set a large heatproof bowl over a saucepan of barely simmering water (do not let the bottom of the bowl touch the water), add the butter and chocolate, and stir frequently until melted and smooth.

Remove the bowl from the heat, add the sugar, salt, and vanilla, and stir until completely combined. Add the eggs one at a time, mixing well after each addition. Add the flour and stir until the batter is smooth, 2 to 3 minutes. Stir in the cocoa nibs.

Pour the batter into the prepared pan and bake for 20 to 22 minutes. When the brownies are done, a slight crack will have formed around the edges. Remove the pan from the oven and let the brownies cool completely on a wire rack.

To make the ganache: Combine the cream, butter, sugar, and salt in a large heatproof bowl, set it over a saucepan of barely simmering water (do not let the bottom of the bowl touch the water), and stir until the butter is melted. Add the chocolate and stir until the chocolate has melted and the mixture is completely smooth.

Remove the bowl from the heat, add the coffee and vanilla, and stir until smooth. The ganache will thicken as it cools.

To finish the brownies: Invert the brownies onto a baking sheet and remove the parchment. Pour the thickened ganache over the brownies, spreading it evenly with a spatula or a butter knife into a thick layer on top. Let the brownies stand until the ganache is completely set and sprinkle with fleur de sel if desired.

Cut the brownies into squares. They will keep in an airtight container at room temperature for up to 1 week.

TIP: Cocoa nibs are seeds of the cocoa plant that are fermented, roasted, and then cracked and separated from the husks, leaving a crunchy texture and a subtle chocolate flavor. They make a great substitute for roasted nuts or chocolate chips in baked goods.

STAR BROWNIES

These rich, melt-in-your-mouth chocolate brownies have been a favorite at the bakery from day one. Back in the day, we hand-mixed the batter, and I always had to count the strokes to make sure it was properly mixed. These days, we make the batter in a stand mixer, but here I give you the counting-strokes method. It's a little tedious, but it's the most reliable method I know, and it makes for a fantastic brownie.

½ POUND (2 STICKS) UNSALTED BUTTER, CUT INTO CUBES

½ POUND UNSWEETENED CHOCOLATE, PREFERABLY SCHARFFEN BERGER 99% CACAO, CHOPPED

2½ CUPS GRANULATED SUGAR

1½ TEASPOONS FINE SEA SALT

1 TABLESPOON PURE VANILLA EXTRACT

4 LARGE EGGS, AT ROOM TEMPERATURE

1 CUP UNBLEACHED ALL-PURPOSE FLOUR

CONFECTIONERS' SUGAR FOR DUSTING (OPTIONAL)

Position a rack in the lower third of the oven and preheat the oven to 350°F. Lightly spray a 9-inch square baking pan with nonstick spray. Line with parchment, leaving an overhang on two opposite sides of the pan.

Set a medium heatproof bowl over a saucepan of simmering water (make sure the bowl does not touch the water), add the butter and chocolate, and stir frequently until melted and smooth.

Remove the bowl from the heat, add the sugar, salt, and vanilla, and stir with a wooden spoon until thoroughly combined. Add one egg and beat it in, counting 100 strokes. Add the remaining eggs one at a time, counting 100 strokes after each one. It's an arm workout, but it wasn't so bad, right?

Add the flour and fold it into the batter until just combined.

Pour the batter into the prepared pan. Bake for 50 to 55 minutes, until a slight crack has formed around the edges. Place the pan on a wire rack and let the brownies cool completely.

Using the parchment "handles," remove the brownies from the pan. Remove the parchment and cut the brownies into 16 squares. You can decorate the top with confectioners' sugar, if you'd like. I use a stencil of a star, of course.

The brownies can be stored in an airtight container at room temperature for up to 5 days.

I like to refrigerate the brownies, which makes them extra chewy and fudgy—yum.

GINGER CAKE SQUARES WITH FRESH WHIPPED CREAM

SERVES 6 OR 8

This recipe has been passed down in my family for at least four generations. My great-grandmother was famous for the homemade ginger cake squares she sold at her general store. This simple recipe is the one she used. We make this at Christmastime, but I crave ginger cake all year long.

½ CUP SUGAR

8 TABLESPOONS (1 STICK) UNSALTED BUTTER, MELTED

1 CUP BLACKSTRAP MOLASSES

1 LARGE EGG

2½ CUPS UNBLEACHED ALL-PURPOSE FLOUR

1½ TEASPOONS BAKING SODA

½ TEASPOON FINE SEA SALT

1 TABLESPOON GROUND GINGER

1½ TEASPOONS GROUND CINNAMON

½ TEASPOON GROUND CLOVES

½ TEASPOON FRESHLY GRATED NUTMEG

½ TEASPOON GROUND ALLSPICE

1 CUP BOILING WATER

¼ CUP CANDIED GINGER, FINELY CHOPPED

1 RECIPE FRESH WHIPPED CREAM (RECIPE FOLLOWS)

Position a rack in the lower third of the oven and preheat the oven to 350°F. Butter an 8-inch square baking pan. Line the bottom with parchment and butter it as well. Lightly dust the pan with flour, tapping the pan on the counter to shake out any excess.

continued

In a medium bowl, whisk the sugar, butter, molasses, and egg together; set aside.

Sift together the flour, baking soda, and salt into a medium mixing bowl. Whisk in the ginger, cinnamon, cloves, nutmeg, and allspice. Stir the dry ingredients into the molasses-egg mixture, then add the boiling water, whisking until well blended. Fold in the candied ginger.

Pour the batter into the prepared pan and bake for 35 to 40 minutes, until a cake tester inserted in the

center of the cake comes out clean. Let the cake cool in the pan for 15 minutes, then remove from the pan and transfer to a wire rack to cool completely while you make the whipped cream.

Cut the ginger cake into 6 or 8 squares and serve warm with the whipped cream.

The cake is even better the next day. The squares can be stored in an airtight container at room temperature for up to 3 days.

Fresh Whipped Cream

MAKES ABOUT 3 CUPS

2 CUPS HEAVY CREAM

¼ CUP CONFECTIONERS' SUGAR

Using a stand mixer fitted with the whisk attachment (or in a large mixing bowl, using a handheld mixer), whip the cream on medium speed until it starts to thicken. Add the confectioners' sugar and beat until the cream holds nice soft peaks. Use the whipped cream immediately.

DRUNK BLONDIES

In the bakery, we give funny little names to all our treats. The customers are as amused by them as we are. Case in point: One day a priest from the neighborhood came into the bakery. He studied the cases, then came up to the counter and said, rather sheepishly, "Can I have a Drunk Blondie and a Hazel Feelgood?"

2 CUPS UNBLEACHED
ALL-PURPOSE FLOUR

1 TEASPOON BAKING POWDER,
PREFERABLY ALUMINUM-FREE

¼ TEASPOON FINE SEA SALT

½ POUND (2 STICKS)
UNSALTED BUTTER, MELTED

2 CUPS PACKED LIGHT
BROWN SUGAR

2 LARGE EGGS,
AT ROOM TEMPERATURE

2 TEASPOONS PURE
VANILLA EXTRACT

2 TABLESPOONS BOURBON

¼ CUP CHOPPED PECANS

½ CUP SWEETENED FLAKED
COCONUT, TOASTED (SEE TIP)

¼ CUP MINI SEMISWEET
CHOCOLATE CHIPS

Position a rack in the middle of the oven and preheat the oven to 350°F. Grease a 9-by-13-inch baking pan and line with parchment, allowing the ends of the paper to hang over two opposite edges of the pan.

In a medium bowl, whisk the flour, baking powder, and salt together; set aside.

Put the butter and brown sugar in a large mixing bowl and stir with a spoon until smooth. Add the eggs, vanilla, and bourbon, and mix until thoroughly combined. Stir in the flour mixture, followed by the pecans, coconut, and chocolate chips.

continued

Pour the batter into the prepared pan and smooth the top with a spatula. Bake for 20 to 25 minutes, until the top is golden brown. Remove the pan from the oven and let cool completely on a wire rack.

Cut the blondies into bars. They will keep in an airtight container at room temperature for up to 3 days.

TIP: The easiest way to toast coconut is in the oven. Position a rack in the lower third of the oven and preheat the oven to 350°F. Spread the coconut in a baking pan and bake for 5 to 8 minutes, tossing every couple of minutes with a heat-resistant spoon to ensure even browning. Keep a close eye on the coconut, because it can burn easily.

PB&J BARS

Who doesn't love a peanut butter and jelly sandwich? So many of us remember our mom packing them into our lunch box. These bars are a delicious treat for school events or parties—kids and grown-ups alike love them.

FOR THE BARS

3 CUPS UNBLEACHED ALL-PURPOSE FLOUR

1½ TEASPOONS BAKING SODA

1 TEASPOON BAKING POWDER, PREFERABLY ALUMINUM-FREE

½ POUND (2 STICKS) UNSALTED BUTTER, AT ROOM TEMPERATURE

1 CUP GRANULATED SUGAR

1 CUP PACKED LIGHT BROWN SUGAR

1 CUP CREAMY PEANUT BUTTER

2 LARGE EGGS

ONE 12-OUNCE JAR STRAWBERRY JAM, OR YOUR FAVORITE FLAVOR

FOR THE GLAZE

2 CUPS CONFECTIONERS' SUGAR

2 TEASPOONS PURE VANILLA EXTRACT

1 TABLESPOON HOT WATER, OR AS NEEDED

Position a rack in the middle of the oven and preheat the oven to 350°F. Grease a 9-by-13-inch baking pan and line with parchment, allowing the ends of the paper to hang over two opposite edges of the pan.

To make the bars: In a medium bowl, whisk the flour, baking soda, and baking powder together. Set aside.

In the bowl of a stand mixer fitted with the paddle attachment (or in a large mixing bowl, using a handheld mixer), cream the butter, both sugars, and peanut butter on medium speed until smooth, about 2 minutes. Add the eggs one at a time, beating well after each addition. Turn the speed down to low and add the flour mixture, mixing until just combined. The dough will resemble cookie dough.

Press two-thirds of the dough evenly over the bottom of the prepared pan. Spread the jam evenly over the dough. Distribute small dollops of the remaining dough evenly over the jam.

Bake for 35 to 45 minutes, until golden brown. The edges will be firm and the center should be set. Remove the bars from the oven and let cool to room temperature on a wire rack.

To make the glaze: Mix the confectioners' sugar, vanilla, and hot water together in a medium bowl until smooth. Add more water if necessary to reach the consistency of a glaze.

Drizzle the bars with the glaze, then cut into squares.

The squares will keep in an airtight container at room temperature for up to 1 week.

PUMPKIN CRUNCH BARS

This alternative to traditional pumpkin pie is silky smooth and warmed with spices and features a shortbread cookie crust. These bars are by far our best seller during the holidays, especially at Thanksgiving. I always have to chuckle, though, when someone asks for them in the middle of the summer.

FOR THE CRUST

½ POUND (2 STICKS) UNSALTED BUTTER

½ CUP SUGAR

1 TEASPOON PURE VANILLA EXTRACT

½ TEASPOON FINE SEA SALT

2 CUPS UNBLEACHED ALL-PURPOSE FLOUR

FOR THE FILLING

ONE 8-OUNCE PACKAGE CREAM CHEESE, AT ROOM TEMPERATURE

ONE 15-OUNCE CAN PUMPKIN PUREE

8 TABLESPOONS (1 STICK) UNSALTED BUTTER, MELTED

1½ TEASPOONS PURE VANILLA EXTRACT

ONE 1-POUND BOX (4 CUPS) CONFECTIONERS' SUGAR

½ TEASPOON GROUND MACE

1 TEASPOON GROUND CINNAMON

1 TEASPOON FRESHLY GRATED NUTMEG

3 LARGE EGGS

1 RECIPE FRESH WHIPPED CREAM, FOR TOPPING (OPTIONAL; PAGE 34)

Position a rack in the middle of the oven and preheat the oven to 350°F. Grease a 9-by-13-inch baking pan and line with parchment, allowing the paper to hang over the edges.

To make the crust: Put the butter in a large heatproof bowl, set it over a pot of barely simmering water, and stir frequently until melted.

continued

Remove from the heat and stir in the sugar, vanilla, and salt. Add the flour all at once and mix until just incorporated.

Press the dough evenly into the bottom of the prepared pan. Bake for 20 to 25 minutes, until golden on the edges but still light brown in the center. Let the crust cool for at least 30 minutes.

To make the filling: In the bowl of a stand mixer fitted with the paddle attachment (or in a medium mixing bowl, using a handheld mixer), beat the cream cheese on medium speed until smooth and creamy, 5 to 7 minutes. Add the pumpkin and mix until thoroughly incorporated, about 5 minutes. Turn the speed to low, add the melted butter and vanilla, and mix until combined, 2 to 3 minutes. Add the confectioners' sugar, mace, cinnamon, nutmeg, and eggs, beating until all the ingredients are thoroughly combined. Continue to mix on medium speed until smooth, about 5 minutes.

Pour into the prepared crust. Bake for 50 minutes to 1 hour, until the center is firm. Let cool to room temperature on a wire rack, then refrigerate.

Cut the bars into squares and serve chilled with the whipped cream, if desired.

The bars will keep in an airtight container in the refrigerator for up to 3 days.

LEMON PIE BARS

This bar with a graham cracker crust has old-school charm. Its creamy, cool texture is refreshing, and it is simple to make. To celebrate St. Patrick's Day, substitute key lime juice and zest for the lemon to make a lime-green pie bar.

FOR THE CRUST

3 CUPS GRAHAM CRACKER CRUMBS (APPROXIMATELY 24 CRACKERS)

12 TABLESPOONS (1½ STICKS) UNSALTED BUTTER, MELTED

2 TABLESPOONS SUGAR

FOR THE FILLING

1 CUP HEAVY CREAM

2 TEASPOONS GRATED LEMON ZEST

1 CUP FRESH LEMON JUICE

TWO 14-OUNCE CANS SWEETENED CONDENSED MILK

6 LARGE EGG YOLKS

1 RECIPE FRESH WHIPPED CREAM (PAGE 34)

Position a rack in the middle of the oven and preheat the oven to 350°F. Grease a 9-by-13-inch baking pan and line with parchment, allowing the ends of the paper to hang over two opposite edges of the pan.

To make the crust: In a medium bowl, combine the graham cracker crumbs, butter, and sugar and blend with a fork until the crumbs are evenly moistened. Press the graham cracker mixture firmly and evenly into the bottom of the prepared pan. Use a piece of parchment to press on the crust with the palms of your hands to make sure it is completely level.

continued

Bake the crust for about 8 minutes, until lightly golden. Let cool completely before adding the filling. Turn the oven temperature down to 325°F.

To make the filling: In a large bowl, whisk the heavy cream, lemon zest, lemon juice, sweetened condensed milk, and egg yolks together. Pour the filling over the cooled crust.

Place the baking pan inside a larger baking pan and pour enough hot water into the larger pan to come halfway up the sides of the smaller pan. Bake for 20 to 25 minutes, until the filling is puffed at the edges and no longer jiggles in the center when the pan is tapped. Remove the pan from the water bath and set it on a rack to cool for 1 hour, then refrigerate until cold.

Cut the bars into squares and serve chilled, with the whipped cream.

The bars will keep in an airtight container in the refrigerator for up to 3 days.

SHAKER MEYER LEMON PIE BARS

The Shakers wasted nothing, and they used whole lemons in this pie bar. That's right—rind, pith, and all go into the filling. Be sure to slice the lemons as thin as you can and let them macerate in sugar for at least 3 hours (the longer, the better). The result is a tart lemony filling similar in texture to marmalade. You can substitute regular lemons, if Meyer lemons are not in season.

FOR THE FILLING

2 LARGE MEYER LEMONS, SCRUBBED

2 CUPS GRANULATED SUGAR

4 LARGE EGGS

¼ TEASPOON FINE SEA SALT

FOR THE CRUST

½ POUND (2 STICKS) UNSALTED BUTTER, MELTED

½ CUP GRANULATED SUGAR

1½ TEASPOONS PURE VANILLA EXTRACT

1½ TEASPOONS FINE SEA SALT

2 CUPS UNBLEACHED ALL-PURPOSE FLOUR

SPECIAL EQUIPMENT

MANDOLINE OR OTHER VEGETABLE SLICER

To prepare the lemons for the filling: Slice the stem ends off the lemons. Using a mandoline, slice the lemons paper-thin and place them in a nonreactive bowl, like glass or stainless steel (do not use aluminum). Pick out and discard all the seeds. Add the sugar to the lemons and toss together with your hands. Cover the bowl with plastic wrap and let sit at room temperature for at least 3 hours, or up to 12 hours. The skin of the lemons

will soften and the sugar will completely dissolve. If you see any seeds floating on top, discard them.

Position a rack in the middle of the oven and preheat the oven to 350°F. Line a 9-inch square baking pan with parchment, letting the ends of the parchment hang over two opposite sides of the pan.

To make the crust: In a medium bowl, stir together the butter, sugar, vanilla, and salt until well blended. Add the flour in thirds and stir until just incorporated.

Press the mixture evenly into the bottom of the prepared pan. Prick the crust all over with a fork. Bake for 15 to 18 minutes, until the crust is golden. Set aside to cool while you make the filling. (Leave the oven on.)

To make the filling: In a small bowl, whisk the eggs and salt together. Add to the lemon mixture and stir to combine.

Pour the filling into the prebaked crust. Bake for 30 to 40 minutes, until golden and the center no longer jiggles. Place on a wire rack to cool, then refrigerate before cutting into 12 bars and serving.

The bars can be stored in an airtight container in the refrigerator for up to 3 days.

CUPCAKES

OLD-FASHIONED CUPCAKES WITH BUTTERCREAM FROSTING

Every time we make these cupcakes, I am six years old all over again and tempted to lick the beaters of the buttery cake batter. We decorate the finished cakes with buttercream and sprinkles in my favorite pastel-toned palette of pink, green, baby blue, and yellow, but they are also the perfect canvas for traditional holiday colors. We haven't tried to reinvent this nostalgic cake, leaving the American classic just as it should be.

1 CUP WHOLE MILK

1 TEASPOON PURE VANILLA EXTRACT

1¾ CUPS CAKE FLOUR (NOT SELF-RISING)

1¼ CUPS UNBLEACHED ALL-PURPOSE FLOUR

2 CUPS SUGAR

1 TABLESPOON BAKING POWDER, PREFERABLY ALUMINUM-FREE

¾ TEASPOON FINE SEA SALT

½ POUND (2 STICKS) UNSALTED BUTTER, CUT INTO ½-INCH CUBES, AT ROOM TEMPERATURE

4 LARGE EGGS, AT ROOM TEMPERATURE

1 RECIPE BUTTERCREAM FROSTING (RECIPE FOLLOWS)

HAND-TINTED SPRINKLES (OPTIONAL; SEE PAGE 57)

Position a rack in the lower third of the oven and preheat the oven to 350°F. Line 24 cupcake cups with paper liners.

In a large measuring cup or a small bowl, mix together the milk and vanilla; set aside.

continued

THE ARTISANAL KITCHEN: *Sweets & Treats*

In the bowl of a stand mixer fitted with the paddle attachment (or in a large mixing bowl, using a handheld mixer), combine both flours, the sugar, baking powder, and salt and mix on low speed for 2 to 3 minutes, until thoroughly combined. With the mixer on low speed, add the butter a few pieces at a time, mixing for about 2 minutes, until the mixture resembles coarse sand.

With the mixer on medium speed, add the eggs one at a time, mixing well after each addition. Turn the speed to low and gradually add the milk and vanilla, then mix for another 1 to 2 minutes.

Remove the bowl from the mixer and, using a rubber spatula, incorporate any ingredients hiding at the bottom of the bowl, making sure the batter is completely mixed.

With a large ice cream scoop or spoon, scoop the batter into the prepared cupcake cups, filling each one about two-thirds full. Bake for 20 to 25 minutes, until a cake tester inserted in the center of a cupcake comes out clean. Let cool for at least 20 minutes.

To frost the cupcakes: Using a spatula or a butter knife, spread the tops of the cupcakes with swirls of frosting. Top with sprinkles, if desired.

The cupcakes can be stored in an airtight container at room temperature for up to 2 days.

TIP: This recipe uses an unusual method for mixing the cake batter that was inspired by Rose Levy Beranbaum's one-bowl method in *The Cake Bible*. Adding the small bits of butter to the dry ingredients is very similar to making a pastry dough. It is a foolproof method for not overmixing the batter, and the result is a tender, delicate cake that is light and fluffy.

Buttercream Frosting

½ POUND (2 STICKS) UNSALTED
BUTTER, AT ROOM TEMPERATURE

6 TO 7 CUPS CONFECTIONERS' SUGAR

½ CUP WHOLE MILK

2 TEASPOONS PURE
VANILLA EXTRACT

LIQUID GEL FOOD COLORING
(OPTIONAL)

In the bowl of a stand mixer fitted
with the paddle attachment (or in a
large mixing bowl, using a handheld mixer), cream the butter on
medium speed until light and fluffy,
2 to 3 minutes. Add 4 cups of the
confectioners' sugar, the milk, and
vanilla and mix on low speed until
smooth and creamy, 2 to 3 minutes.

Gradually add up to 3 cups more
confectioners' sugar, mixing on low
speed, until the frosting reaches the
desired light and fluffy consistency,
3 to 5 minutes.

If desired, to tint the frosting, add
a drop or two of food coloring to
the frosting, mixing well; add more
coloring as necessary until you
reach the desired shade. If you want
multiple colors, scoop the frosting
into several bowls, then add the food
coloring.

The frosting can be stored in
an airtight container at room
temperature for up to 2 days.

HAND-TINTED SPRINKLES

Sprinkles add a touch of fun and color to the tops of cupcakes. We hand-tint our sprinkles in the same shades of pink, blue, green, and yellow that we frost the cupcakes, using the simple technique my mother taught me. You can also use traditional holiday colors and add a sparkle to your next party.

To tint sprinkles, pour white sprinkles into a Mason jar or a ziplock bag and add a pinch (it doesn't take much) of powdered food coloring (see Resources, page 104). Screw on the lid and shake, shake, shake until the sprinkles take on the desired shade, adding more powder if necessary. Store the jar of sprinkles in a cool place and use as desired. To decorate a kitchen shelf, fill multiple jars with sprinkles of different colors.

SWEET POTATO CUPCAKES WITH CARAMEL CREAM CHEESE FROSTING

In the South, we eat sweet potatoes all year long, not just at Thanksgiving. This cupcake offers the same spicy, brown-sugary goodness of the side dish with the toasted marshmallows, but in a sweet handheld package. If you don't have a kitchen blowtorch, just toast the marshmallows over an open flame on your stove and pop them on top of the cupcakes.

2 CUPS UNBLEACHED
ALL-PURPOSE FLOUR

2¼ TEASPOONS BAKING POWDER,
PREFERABLY ALUMINUM-FREE

¾ TEASPOON BAKING SODA

1 TEASPOON FINE SEA SALT

1 TEASPOON GROUND GINGER

1 TEASPOON GROUND CINNAMON

½ TEASPOON GROUND CLOVES

½ TEASPOON GROUND MACE

¼ TEASPOON GROUND CARDAMOM

1¼ CUPS PACKED LIGHT BROWN SUGAR

4 LARGE EGGS,
AT ROOM TEMPERATURE

1 CUP VEGETABLE OIL

1 POUND SWEET POTATOES
(1 TO 2 SWEET POTATOES),
BAKED AND COOLED, FLESH
SCRAPED OUT AND MASHED

1 TABLESPOON GRATED
ORANGE ZEST

½ CUP WHOLE MILK

1 RECIPE CARAMEL CREAM CHEESE
FROSTING (RECIPE FOLLOWS)

LARGE OR MINI MARSHMALLOWS
(OPTIONAL)

SPECIAL EQUIPMENT

KITCHEN BLOWTORCH

Position a rack in the lower third of the oven and preheat the oven to 350°F. Line 24 cupcake cups with paper liners.

Sift together the flour, baking powder, baking soda, salt, ginger, cinnamon, cloves, mace, and cardamom; set aside.

In the bowl of a stand mixer fitted with the paddle attachment (or in a large mixing bowl, using a handheld mixer), beat the brown sugar and eggs on medium speed for 3 to 4 minutes, until pale and fluffy. Add the oil, sweet potatoes, and orange zest, beating just until incorporated.

With the mixer on low speed, add the flour mixture in thirds, alternating with the milk, beginning and ending with the dry ingredients.

Remove the bowl from the mixer and, using a rubber spatula, incorporate any ingredients hiding at the bottom of the bowl, making sure the batter is completely mixed. With a large ice cream scoop or spoon, scoop the batter into the prepared cupcake cups, filling each one about two-thirds full. Bake for 20 to 25 minutes, until a cake tester inserted in the center of a cupcake comes out clean. Let cool for at least 20 minutes.

To assemble the cupcakes: Using a spatula or a butter knife, spread the tops of the cupcakes with swirls of the frosting and decorate with marshmallows, if using. With a kitchen blowtorch, lightly toast the marshmallows, being careful not to burn the paper liners.

The cupcakes can be stored in an airtight container at room temperature for up to 2 days.

Caramel Cream Cheese Frosting

FOR THE CARAMEL

1 CUP GRANULATED SUGAR

12 TABLESPOONS (1½ STICKS) UNSALTED BUTTER, AT ROOM TEMPERATURE

2 TABLESPOONS HEAVY CREAM

FOR THE FROSTING

TWO 8-OUNCE PACKAGES CREAM CHEESE, CUT INTO ½-INCH CUBES, AT ROOM TEMPERATURE

4 TABLESPOONS UNSALTED BUTTER, AT ROOM TEMPERATURE

1 TEASPOON PURE VANILLA EXTRACT

2 CUPS CONFECTIONERS' SUGAR

To make the caramel: Combine the granulated sugar and ¼ cup water in a medium saucepan and cook over medium-high heat, stirring, until the sugar is completely dissolved. Using a wet pastry brush, wash down any crystals from the sides of the pan. Turn the heat down to medium and continue to cook, without stirring, until the syrup becomes a medium-dark amber color, about 10 minutes; you can carefully swirl the pan around to check the color.

Remove the pan from the heat and immediately stir in the butter and heavy cream (be careful of the hot steam!). Do not worry if the butter starts to separate; it will come together once the caramel is cooled.

Transfer the caramel to the bowl of a stand mixer fitted with the whisk attachment (or to a medium mixing bowl, if using a handheld mixer) and beat on low speed until the caramel cools and starts to come together. Transfer the caramel to a small bowl.

To make the frosting: Beat the cream cheese, butter, and vanilla in a large bowl with a handheld mixer on medium speed until smooth, 2 to 3 minutes. With the mixer on low speed, gradually add the confectioners' sugar, beating until light and fluffy. Add the caramel and continue to beat until smooth and creamy, 4 to 5 minutes.

BANANA–CHOCOLATE CHIP CUPCAKES WITH CHOCOLATE CREAM CHEESE FROSTING

MAKES 24 CUPCAKES

When I was a child, we used to buy frozen bananas dipped in chocolate on the Santa Monica Pier. Ever since, I've loved how the two flavors go together. These cupcakes are based on chiffon cake, so popular with America's home bakers throughout the 1940s and '50s.

2 CUPS CAKE FLOUR (NOT SELF-RISING)

1⅓ CUPS SUGAR

1 TEASPOON BAKING POWDER, PREFERABLY ALUMINUM-FREE

1 TEASPOON BAKING SODA

1 TEASPOON FINE SEA SALT

2 LARGE EGGS, SEPARATED

1 LARGE EGG WHITE

¼ TEASPOON CREAM OF TARTAR

¾ CUP BUTTERMILK

⅓ CUP CANOLA OIL

1 TEASPOON PURE VANILLA EXTRACT

1 CUP MASHED RIPE BANANAS (ABOUT 2½ LARGE BANANAS)

½ CUP SEMISWEET CHOCOLATE CHIPS

1 RECIPE CHOCOLATE CREAM CHEESE FROSTING (RECIPE FOLLOWS)

Position a rack in the lower third of the oven and preheat the oven to 350°F. Line 24 cupcake cups with paper liners.

In a large mixing bowl, sift together the cake flour, 1 cup of the sugar, the baking powder, baking soda, and salt; set aside.

In the bowl of a stand mixer fitted with the whisk attachment (or in a large mixing bowl, using a handheld mixer), beat the egg whites and cream of tartar until frothy.

Gradually add the remaining ⅓ cup sugar and continue to whip until stiff peaks form. Set aside.

Make a well in the center of the dry ingredients. Add half of the buttermilk, the oil, vanilla, and mashed bananas and stir for 1 to 2 minutes, until the ingredients are thoroughly combined. Add the egg yolks and the rest of the buttermilk, stirring until just combined. Gently fold in the egg whites and then the chocolate chips.

With a large ice cream scoop or spoon, scoop the batter into the prepared cupcake cups, filling each one about two-thirds full. Bake for 20 to 25 minutes, until a cake tester inserted in the center of a cupcake comes out clean. Let cool.

To frost the cupcakes: Using a spatula or a butter knife, spread the tops of the cupcakes with swirls of the frosting.

The cupcakes can be stored in an airtight container at room temperature for up to 2 days.

Chocolate Cream Cheese Frosting

MAKES ABOUT 3 CUPS

1 CUP SEMISWEET CHOCOLATE CHIPS

¼ CUP HEAVY CREAM

ONE 8-OUNCE PACKAGE CREAM CHEESE, AT ROOM TEMPERATURE

½ CUP CONFECTIONERS' SUGAR

Put the semisweet chocolate chips and heavy cream in a heatproof bowl set over a pot of barely simmering water (do not let the bottom of the bowl touch the water) and stir until the chocolate is melted and smooth. Remove the chocolate from the heat.

In the bowl of a stand mixer fitted with the paddle attachment (or in a large mixing bowl, using a handheld mixer), cream the cream cheese and confectioners' sugar on low speed until smooth. Gradually add the chocolate mixture and mix well.

PINKIES CHOCOLATE
LUNCH-BOX TREATS

Remember those Hostess Sno Balls your mom used to pack in your lunch box? The ones with marshmallow covered in bright pink coconut? This is our updated interpretation.

1½ CUPS CAKE FLOUR
(NOT SELF-RISING)

2 CUPS SUGAR

¾ TEASPOON BAKING SODA

½ TEASPOON FINE SEA SALT

4 OUNCES UNSWEETENED
CHOCOLATE, FINELY CHOPPED

1 CUP HOT FRESHLY BREWED COFFEE

1½ TEASPOONS PURE
VANILLA EXTRACT

2 LARGE EGGS,
AT ROOM TEMPERATURE

½ CUP CANOLA OIL

½ CUP SOUR CREAM, AT ROOM
TEMPERATURE

1 RECIPE COCONUT BUTTERCREAM
(RECIPE FOLLOWS)

FOR THE TINTED COCONUT

4 CUPS SWEETENED FLAKED COCONUT

POWDERED FOOD COLORING
(SEE RESOURCES, PAGE 104)

Position a rack in the lower third of the oven and preheat the oven to 350°F. Line 18 cupcake cups with paper liners.

In the bowl of a stand mixer fitted with the paddle attachment (or in a large mixing bowl, using a handheld mixer), combine the flour, sugar, baking soda, and salt. Let the mixer run on low speed for 2 to 3 minutes to aerate the flour.

Meanwhile, put the chocolate in a medium bowl and pour in the hot coffee and vanilla. Let the mixture stand for about 2 minutes to melt the chocolate, then stir until smooth.

In another medium bowl, whisk the eggs and oil together until thick, satiny, and light in color. Whisk in the sour cream, being careful not to overmix; leave some visible streaks of white. Pour in the melted chocolate mixture and mix until just combined.

Add the chocolate–sour cream mixture to the dry ingredients in thirds, mixing on medium speed for 1 to 2 minutes, until just combined.

Remove the bowl from the mixer and, using a rubber spatula, incorporate any ingredients hiding at the bottom of the bowl, making sure the batter is completely mixed. The batter will be very runny, so it's best to transfer it to a large liquid measuring cup to make it easier to pour.

Pour the batter into the prepared cupcake cups, filling each one about two-thirds full. Bake for 20 to 25 minutes, until a cake tester inserted in the center of a cupcake comes out clean. Let cool for at least 20 minutes. Once the cupcakes are cool, remove them from the liners.

To assemble the cupcakes: Use an apple corer or a paring knife to scoop out a hole in the middle of each cupcake, about 1 inch deep. (The extra cake is yours for the snacking!)

Fill a pastry bag fitted with a ½-inch or larger tip with the frosting and fill the holes in each cupcake with frosting. Arrange the cupcakes on a baking sheet lined with parchment or foil and refrigerate for at least 15 minutes to set the frosting.

To make the tinted coconut: Put the coconut in a Mason jar or a ziplock bag. Add a few pinches of food coloring, one at a time, and shake until the coconut is evenly colored.

Once the frosting in the centers of the cupcakes sets, frost the tops and sides of the cupcakes with the remaining frosting. Put the coconut in a small bowl, roll the frosted cupcakes in the coconut, and place them in paper liners.

The cupcakes can be stored in an airtight container at room temperature for up to 2 days.

Coconut Buttercream

½ CUP ALL-PURPOSE FLOUR

2 CUPS WHOLE MILK

2 TEASPOONS PURE
VANILLA EXTRACT

2 TEASPOONS COCONUT EXTRACT

1 POUND (4 STICKS) UNSALTED BUTTER,
AT ROOM TEMPERATURE

2 CUPS CONFECTIONERS' SUGAR

Combine the flour, ¼ cup of the milk, the vanilla, and the coconut extract in a small saucepan and whisk until blended. Set the pan over medium heat and gradually add the remaining 1¾ cups milk, whisking constantly. Cook the mixture, whisking, until it comes to a low boil, then reduce the heat to low and continue to whisk until the mixture begins to thicken and starts to "burp," 2 to 3 minutes.

Transfer the mixture to a small heatproof bowl and stir it occasionally as it cools to keep it lump-free. If you do get a few lumps, don't worry—you can whisk the mixture to dissolve the lumps, or pass it through a fine-mesh sieve. Cool to room temperature. (You can put it in the refrigerator for 10 minutes to speed up the process.)

In the bowl of a stand mixer fitted with the whisk attachment (or in a large bowl, using a handheld mixer), whip the butter on medium speed until soft and creamy, 2 to 3 minutes. Gradually add the confectioners' sugar and beat on high speed until light and fluffy, 5 to 7 minutes.

Gradually add the milk mixture, then increase the speed to medium-high and whip until the frosting is light and fluffy, scraping down the bottom and sides of the bowl as necessary with a rubber spatula to make sure the frosting is thoroughly mixed.

The frosting can be stored in an airtight container at room temperature for up to 2 days.

GINGERBREAD CUPCAKES WITH LEMON–CREAM CHEESE FROSTING

MAKES 24 CUPCAKES

The snap of spice and the warmth of gingerbread always make it the treat of choice for me on a cool fall day. When topped with a lemony frosting, these gingerbread cupcakes get a fresh burst of flavor. During the holidays, I like to deck these out with decorated mini sugar cookies made from scraps of dough for festive treats. For an added bonus, when you bake these, the aroma of ginger, cinnamon, and allspice will fill your kitchen with holiday cheer.

3 CUPS UNBLEACHED
ALL-PURPOSE FLOUR

1½ TEASPOONS GROUND GINGER

1 TEASPOON BAKING SODA

1 TEASPOON GROUND CINNAMON

½ TEASPOON FINE SEA SALT

½ TEASPOON GROUND ALLSPICE

½ POUND (2 STICKS) UNSALTED
BUTTER, AT ROOM TEMPERATURE

1 CUP PACKED LIGHT BROWN SUGAR

4 LARGE EGGS,
AT ROOM TEMPERATURE

1 CUP BUTTERMILK

2 TABLESPOONS LIGHT UNSULFURED
MOLASSES

2 TEASPOONS PURE VANILLA EXTRACT

1 RECIPE LEMON–CREAM CHEESE
FROSTING (RECIPE FOLLOWS)

Position a rack in the middle of the oven and preheat the oven to 350°F. Line 24 cupcake cups with paper liners.

Sift together the flour, ginger, baking soda, cinnamon, salt, and allspice. Set aside.

In the bowl of a stand mixer fitted with the paddle attachment (or in a large mixing bowl, using a handheld mixer), cream the butter and brown sugar on medium-high speed for 3 to 5 minutes, until light and fluffy. Turn the mixer speed down to low and add the eggs one at a time, beating well after each addition and scraping down the sides of the bowl with a rubber spatula as necessary.

With the mixer on low speed, add the flour mixture in three additions, alternating with the buttermilk and beginning and ending with the flour, mixing just until incorporated. Add the molasses and vanilla.

Remove the bowl from the mixer and, using a rubber spatula, incorporate any ingredients hiding at the bottom of the bowl, making sure the batter is completely mixed. With a large ice cream scoop or spoon, scoop the batter into the prepared cupcake cups, filling each one about two-thirds full.

Bake for 20 to 25 minutes, until a cake tester inserted in the center of a cupcake comes out clean. Let cool for 15 minutes in the pans, then remove from the pans and cool completely on a wire rack.

To frost the cupcakes: Use a spatula or a butter knife to spread the tops of the cupcakes generously with the cream cheese frosting.

The cupcakes can be refrigerated for up to 2 days. Bring to room temperature before serving.

continued

Lemon–Cream Cheese Frosting

TWO 8-OUNCE PACKAGES CREAM CHEESE, AT ROOM TEMPERATURE

8 TABLESPOONS (1 STICK) UNSALTED BUTTER, AT ROOM TEMPERATURE

2 TEASPOONS GRATED LEMON ZEST

1 TABLESPOON FRESH LEMON JUICE

5 TO 6 CUPS CONFECTIONERS' SUGAR

In the bowl of a stand mixer fitted with the paddle attachment (or in a large bowl, using a handheld mixer), beat the cream cheese, butter, lemon zest, and lemon juice on medium speed until smooth and creamy, 2 to 3 minutes. Gradually add 5 cups of the confectioners' sugar, then add up to 1 cup more sugar if the frosting seems thin, and beat on high speed until light and fluffy, 5 to 7 minutes.

The frosting can be used immediately or covered and refrigerated for up to 5 days.

COCONUT CUPCAKES WITH WHIPPED BUTTERCREAM FROSTING

These coconut cupcakes are one of Griff's favorite treats. He loves the tender sweetness of coconut on top of the lightest buttercream frosting this side of the Mississippi. The hint of cardamom in the batter adds a delicate floral flavor.

3 CUPS UNBLEACHED ALL-PURPOSE FLOUR

1 TEASPOON BAKING POWDER, PREFERABLY ALUMINUM-FREE

½ TEASPOON BAKING SODA

1½ TEASPOONS FINE SEA SALT

½ TEASPOON GROUND CARDAMOM

¾ POUND (3 STICKS) UNSALTED BUTTER, AT ROOM TEMPERATURE

2 CUPS GRANULATED SUGAR

5 LARGE EGGS, AT ROOM TEMPERATURE

1 TEASPOON PURE VANILLA EXTRACT

1 CUP BUTTERMILK

2¾ CUPS SWEETENED FLAKED COCONUT

1 RECIPE WHIPPED BUTTERCREAM FROSTING (RECIPE FOLLOWS)

Position a rack in the middle of the oven and preheat the oven to 350°F. Line 24 cupcake cups with paper liners.

Sift together the flour, baking powder, baking soda, salt, and cardamom. Set aside.

In the bowl of a stand mixer fitted with the paddle attachment (or in a large mixing bowl, using a handheld mixer), cream the butter and sugar on medium-high speed for 3 to 5 minutes, until light and fluffy. Turn the mixer speed down to low and add the eggs one at a time, beating well after each addition, and

scraping down the sides of the bowl with a rubber spatula as necessary. Add the vanilla and mix until combined.

On low speed, add the flour mixture in thirds, alternating with the buttermilk and beginning and ending with the flour, mixing until just incorporated.

Remove the bowl from the mixer and, using a rubber spatula, incorporate any ingredients hiding at the bottom of the bowl, making sure the batter is completely mixed. Fold in ¾ cup of the coconut.

With a large ice cream scoop or spoon, scoop the batter into the prepared cupcake cups, filling them about two-thirds full. Bake for 20 to 25 minutes, until a cake tester inserted in the center of a cupcake comes out clean. Let cool for 20 minutes in the pans, then remove from the pans and cool completely on a wire rack.

To frost the cupcakes: Use a spatula or a butter knife to spread the tops of the cupcakes generously with the buttercream. Put the remaining 2 cups coconut in a medium bowl and dunk the tops of the cupcakes in coconut to cover.

The cupcakes can be stored in an airtight container at room temperature for up to 2 days.

continued

Whipped Buttercream Frosting

¼ CUP UNBLEACHED
ALL-PURPOSE FLOUR

1 CUP WHOLE MILK

½ POUND (2 STICKS) UNSALTED
BUTTER, AT ROOM TEMPERATURE

1 TEASPOON PURE
VANILLA EXTRACT

1 CUP GRANULATED SUGAR

Combine the flour and ¼ cup of the milk in a small heavy saucepan and whisk until blended. Set the pan over medium heat and gradually add the remaining ¾ cup milk, whisking constantly, then cook, whisking, until the mixture comes to a low boil. Reduce the heat to low and whisk until the mixture begins to thicken and starts to "burp," 2 to 3 minutes.

Transfer the mixture to a small heatproof bowl and stir occasionally as it cools to keep it lump-free. If you do get a few lumps, don't worry—you can whisk the mixture to dissolve the lumps, or pass it

through a fine-mesh sieve. Cool to room temperature. (You can put the mixture in the refrigerator for 10 minutes to speed up the cooling process.)

In the bowl of a stand mixer fitted with the whisk attachment (or in a large bowl, using a handheld mixer), whip the butter and vanilla on medium speed until soft and creamy, 2 to 3 minutes. Gradually add the sugar and then beat on high speed until the mixture is light and fluffy, 5 to 7 minutes.

Reduce the speed to low and gradually add the milk mixture, then increase the speed to medium-high and whip until the frosting is light and fluffy, scraping down the sides of the bowl with a rubber spatula as necessary.

Use the frosting immediately. Or store in an airtight container in the refrigerator for up to 2 days. To use buttercream that has been chilled, see the Tip.

TIP: To use buttercream that has been chilled, remove it from the refrigerator and bring it to room temperature. Make sure that it is softened to room temperature before you use it; if the butter is too cold, the buttercream will break and be a hot mess! Transfer the buttercream to the bowl of a stand mixer fitted with the paddle attachment (or to a large bowl if using a handheld mixer) and beat on medium speed until soft and spreadable, 2 to 3 minutes.

CANDIES

BITTERSWEET PECAN-DULCE DE LECHE TRUFFLES

MAKES 30 TRUFFLES

Have I mentioned my love for pecans? When Griff and I found out that there are actual truffles, called pecan truffles, growing in the soil around the pecan trees of southern Georgia, it was a lightbulb moment. These intensely rich truffles are the perfect hostess gift or addition to a festive dessert table.

¾ CUP PECAN HALVES

FOR THE GANACHE

8 OUNCES BITTERSWEET CHOCOLATE, FINELY CHOPPED

¾ CUP HEAVY CREAM

2 TABLESPOONS UNSALTED BUTTER

3 TABLESPOONS DULCE DE LECHE LIQUEUR, SUCH AS DULSEDA

2 TABLESPOONS DUTCH-PROCESSED COCOA POWDER, FOR COATING

Position a rack in the middle of the oven and preheat the oven to 350°F.

Spread the pecan halves in a single layer on a baking sheet and bake for 5 to 6 minutes, until lightly toasted. Remove the pan from the oven and let the pecans cool completely.

Finely chop the pecans; set aside.

To make the ganache: Put the chocolate in a medium bowl; set aside. Combine the cream and butter in a small saucepan and bring to just under a boil over medium heat, stirring to melt the butter. Remove the cream mixture from the heat, pour it over the chocolate, and allow to stand for 5 minutes.

Stir the ganache gently with a spoon until it is smooth and glossy. Add the liqueur and ⅓ cup of the chopped pecans and stir to combine. Cover the ganache with plastic wrap and refrigerate until firm, about 4 hours.

To make the coating: Combine the remaining chopped pecans and the cocoa powder in a small bowl, stirring to mix thoroughly.

To make the truffles: Line a baking sheet with parchment. Scoop up the ganache with a small melon baller to form imperfect balls, roll the balls in the pecans and cocoa powder to coat, and place on the prepared baking sheet. Cover with plastic wrap and refrigerate until the truffles firm up, at least 1 hour.

To store the truffles, layer them between sheets of wax paper or parchment in an airtight container and refrigerate for up to 2 weeks.

To serve, bring the truffles to room temperature.

BROWN SUGAR FUDGE

This rich brown sugar cousin to chocolate fudge has a nice velvety texture and a delicious balance of sweet and salty.

2 CUPS PACKED LIGHT BROWN SUGAR

1 CUP GRANULATED SUGAR

1 CUP HEAVY CREAM

2 TABLESPOONS LIGHT CORN SYRUP

¼ TEASPOON FINE SEA SALT

2 TABLESPOONS UNSALTED BUTTER

1 TEASPOON PURE VANILLA EXTRACT

½ CUP PECAN PIECES (OPTIONAL)

SPECIAL EQUIPMENT

CANDY THERMOMETER

Butter an 8-inch square baking pan.

In a medium saucepan, combine the brown sugar, granulated sugar, heavy cream, corn syrup, and salt and heat over medium heat, stirring to dissolve the sugar. Insert a candy thermometer and cook, stirring occasionally, until the mixture reaches 238°F (this is the "soft ball stage"), 10 to 15 minutes.

Add the butter and stir until melted and fully incorporated, then remove the pan from the heat and let the mixture stand, without stirring, until it cools to lukewarm (about 120°F).

Add the vanilla to the fudge and beat with a wooden spoon until smooth and creamy. If desired, fold in the nuts. Pour the fudge into the prepared pan and let cool to room temperature.

Once the fudge has set, cut it into squares. Store in an airtight container at room temperature for up to 2 weeks.

LEMON BUTTERMILK FUDGE

MAKES 16 PIECES

My grandma Hannah loved fudge and usually made the chocolate-nutty kind, but on occasion, she would use the last bit of buttermilk in the jug to make buttermilk fudge. I like to add a bit of lemon zest to complement the sweet tanginess of the buttermilk.

½ CUP PECAN PIECES

2 CUPS GRANULATED SUGAR

1 CUP BUTTERMILK

8 TABLESPOONS (1 STICK)
UNSALTED BUTTER,
CUT INTO CUBES

1 TABLESPOON HONEY

⅛ TEASPOON FINE SEA SALT

GRATED ZEST OF 1 LEMON

FLAKY SEA SALT, SUCH AS JACOBSEN
OR MALDON, FOR SPRINKLING
(OPTIONAL)

SPECIAL EQUIPMENT

CANDY THERMOMETER

Preheat the oven to 350°F. Line an 8-inch square baking pan with parchment, leaving an overhang on two opposite sides of the pan.

Spread the pecans in a pie pan and toast in the oven for about 5 minutes, until fragrant. Set aside and turn off the oven.

In a medium saucepan, combine the sugar, buttermilk, butter, honey, and fine sea salt and cook over medium-high heat, stirring occasionally, until the butter has melted and the sugar has dissolved. When the mixture comes to a boil, brush the sides of the saucepan with a pastry brush dipped in water, to remove any sugar crystals; do not stir again. Reduce the heat, insert a candy thermometer, and simmer, without stirring, until the thermometer reaches 238°F (this is the "soft ball stage"), 10 to 15 minutes. The fudge will be pale golden and smell of toffee.

Pour the mixture into the bowl of a stand mixer fitted with the paddle attachment (or use a medium mixing bowl and a handheld mixer). Turn the mixer on to medium-high speed and beat, scraping down the sides of the bowl, until the fudge is thickened, stiff, and matte, 5 to 8 minutes.

Add the toasted pecans and lemon zest and mix until combined. The fudge may break up when you add these ingredients, but continue to mix, and it will become smooth again.

Transfer the fudge to the prepared pan and use an offset spatula to smooth the top. Sprinkle with flakes of sea salt, if desired. Let set for at least an hour, then remove from the pan, and cut into squares.

The fudge can be stored in an airtight container at room temperature for up to 1 week.

VANILLA MARSHMALLOWS

Marshmallows are enjoyed all year round (think s'mores!), but marshmallow season in the bakery is from October through February. Our customers love them in our hot chocolate or just by themselves as a snack. You can make flavored marshmallows using this recipe as the foundation; just replace the vanilla extract with your favorite flavor.

3 CUPS GRANULATED SUGAR

1¼ CUPS LIGHT CORN SYRUP

¼ TEASPOON FINE SEA SALT

4 ENVELOPES UNFLAVORED GELATIN

4 TEASPOONS PURE VANILLA EXTRACT

2 CUPS CONFECTIONERS' SUGAR

SPECIAL EQUIPMENT

CANDY THERMOMETER

Spray a 9-by-13-inch baking pan lightly with nonstick spray, then coat the pan generously with confectioners' sugar.

In a large saucepan, stir ¾ cup water, the granulated sugar, corn syrup, and salt over medium heat until the sugar is dissolved. Insert a candy thermometer and, without stirring, bring to a boil, then cook until the mixture reaches 240°F, about 10 minutes.

Meanwhile, pour ¾ cup water into the bowl of a stand mixer fitted with the whisk attachment (or use a large mixing bowl and a handheld mixer), sprinkle the gelatin over the top, and stir on low speed so that the gelatin softens.

With the mixer on low speed, gradually pour the hot sugar mixture into the gelatin mixture, then blend, gradually increasing the speed to high, until the mixture is fluffy and stiff, 10 to 12 minutes. Turn the speed to low, add the vanilla, and mix to incorporate.

Pour the mixture into the prepared pan and smooth the top with a rubber spatula that has been sprayed with nonstick spray. Let the marshmallow sit at room temperature for 4 to 6 hours, until firm.

Fill a bowl with 2 cups confectioners' sugar. Invert the pan onto a smooth work surface and unmold the marshmallow. Lightly coat a serrated knife with nonstick spray, then cut the marshmallow into 12 or 24 squares, depending on your preference. Pull apart the squares and toss each marshmallow in the confectioners' sugar to coat all over.

Store in an airtight container for up to 1 week.

VARIATIONS

Peppermint Marshmallows: Substitute 1 teaspoon peppermint extract for the vanilla.

Chocolate Marshmallows: Substitute chocolate extract for the vanilla, and add 3 tablespoons Dutch-processed cocoa powder along with the chocolate extract.

COTTON CANDY MERINGUES

MAKES 12 MERINGUES

These sweet confections are light and airy, with a delightful chewy texture. Made with egg whites and sugar, and without flour, they are the perfect treats for gluten-free friends. I like to tint these cookies in pastel shades to match our cupcakes.

4 LARGE EGG WHITES, AT ROOM TEMPERATURE

¼ TEASPOON CREAM OF TARTAR

1 CUP GRANULATED SUGAR

2 TEASPOONS CORNSTARCH

1 TEASPOON WHITE WINE VINEGAR

1½ TEASPOONS PURE VANILLA EXTRACT

LIQUID GEL FOOD COLORING (OPTIONAL)

SPECIAL EQUIPMENT

ONE 3-INCH ROUND COOKIE CUTTER

Position a rack in the lower third of the oven and preheat the oven to 250°F. Line a baking sheet with parchment. Using a 3-inch round cookie cutter as a guide, trace 12 circles at least 1 inch apart on the parchment, then turn the parchment over to use these circles as your guide.

In the bowl of a stand mixer fitted with the whisk attachment (or in a large mixing bowl, using a handheld mixer), whip the egg whites and cream of tartar on high speed until the whites form soft peaks. Gradually add the sugar and cornstarch, then whip until the meringue forms stiff, shiny peaks.

Remove the bowl from the mixer and gently fold in the vinegar and vanilla. Fold in a few drops of food coloring, if using.

Using a large spoon, gently scoop mounds of meringue, about 2 inches high, onto the traced circles on the prepared baking sheet. Smooth the sides with a butter knife.

Bake the meringues for 1¼ to 1½ hours, until they are set to the touch. Turn the oven off and let the meringues cool in the oven for 1½ hours.

The meringues can be stored in an airtight container at room temperature for up to 5 days.

BUTTER MINTS

Every spring, my mother would make these precious little mints, tinting them like colored Easter eggs in all my favorite pastel shades. They look lovely sitting in a candy dish, or you can fill clear cellophane bags with these mints and give them as party favors or hostess gifts. For more creative ways to package Butter Mints and other sweets, see page 94.

8 TABLESPOONS (1 STICK) UNSALTED BUTTER, AT ROOM TEMPERATURE

1 TEASPOON FINE SEA SALT

7 CUPS CONFECTIONERS' SUGAR, SIFTED

⅔ CUP SWEETENED CONDENSED MILK

1 TABLESPOON PEPPERMINT EXTRACT

LIQUID GEL FOOD COLORING— CHOOSE FOUR COLORS

Line a 9-by-13-inch baking pan with parchment.

In the bowl of a stand mixer fitted with the paddle attachment (or in a large mixing bowl, using a handheld mixer), cream the butter and salt together on medium speed for

2 minutes. Add the confectioners' sugar, sweetened condensed milk, and peppermint extract, turn the speed to low, and mix until the mixture gathers into a ball.

Remove the mixture from the bowl, divide it into 4 portions, and form each one into a ball. To color the mixture, add 1 drop of food coloring to one portion, kneading to incorporate it evenly, then add more drops as necessary to darken the shade, kneading to incorporate the color thoroughly. Repeat with the remaining 3 portions, using a different color for each.

One at a time, lay each portion on a work surface lightly dusted with confectioners' sugar and roll by hand into a 1-inch-thick rope. Using a paring knife, cut into 1-inch-thick pieces. Layer the mints between sheets of wax or parchment paper in the prepared pan.

Cover the mints with plastic wrap and refrigerate for at least 4 hours.

The mints will keep refrigerated in an airtight container for up to 1 week.

PECAN BRITTLE

MAKES ½ POUND

While we have many peanut farms in Georgia, we are also blessed with an abundance of pecans. And since we also have a number of customers with peanut allergies (including me!), Griff adapted a traditional peanut brittle recipe, using pecans instead. This brittle has the same crackle as the original, but the pecans impart a deeper, warmer flavor.

2 CUPS SUGAR

1 CUP LIGHT CORN SYRUP

2 CUPS PECAN HALVES, TOASTED

½ TEASPOON FINE SEA SALT

2 TABLESPOONS UNSALTED BUTTER

1 TEASPOON PURE VANILLA EXTRACT

½ TEASPOON BAKING SODA

SPECIAL EQUIPMENT

CANDY THERMOMETER

Generously butter a baking sheet.

In a large heavy saucepan, combine the sugar, corn syrup, and 1 cup water and stir over medium-high heat until the sugar dissolves. Insert a candy thermometer and cook, without stirring, until the sugar syrup reaches 238°F. Add the pecans and salt and stir until the mixture reaches 300°F. Immediately remove the brittle from the heat and stir in the butter, vanilla, and baking soda.

Pour the brittle onto the prepared baking sheet and spread it evenly with a heatproof spatula. Let cool completely.

Break the brittle into bite-sized pieces. Store in an airtight container for up to 2 weeks.

CLEVER IDEAS
FOR PACKAGING FOOD GIFTS

When it comes to vintage treasures, I am like a magpie collecting all of my favorite things. Griff and I both enjoy scouring the flea markets and shops around Savannah and elsewhere during our travels.

We share our great finds with others by using our vintage trinkets to package gifts of cookies and confections. Tall clear jars such as antique battery jars, biscuit jars, and even Mason jars are great for holding handmade treats. Blow up an image of one of your favorite recipe cards and wrap it around the jar, then finish it off with a fun tea towel tied with ribbon.

Look for small picnic baskets, colorful old bread boxes, vintage cake carriers, or little suitcases. Filled with your homemade goods, these make great gifts. You might want to tuck in an unscented votive candle set in a bone china teacup. Teacups make great tea-light holders to create a dim glow at an evening picnic or on a table in the kitchen. Use pretty fluted paper cups to hold separate stacks of cookies and clusters of truffles in a vintage biscuit tin.

Throughout the year, collect vintage boxes and tins, and keep a stash of ribbon on hand for unexpected occasions or guests. Fill the tin with something homemade, and your recipient will have a sweet to snack on and a keepsake to cherish or pass on to someone they love.

SALTED CARAMEL POPCORN

Warning: this stuff is addictive! Back up, Jack—homemade caramel-coated popcorn is so much better than anything out of a box. You can even hide a fun holiday-inspired prize at the bottom of each serving if you like.

10 CUPS POPPED CORN
(ABOUT ⅓ CUP UNPOPPED KERNELS)

1 CUP PACKED LIGHT
BROWN SUGAR

¼ CUP LIGHT CORN SYRUP

6 TABLESPOONS UNSALTED BUTTER

¼ TEASPOON FINE SEA SALT

1 TABLESPOON PURE
VANILLA EXTRACT

½ TEASPOON BAKING SODA

1½ CUPS WHOLE ALMONDS

1 TEASPOON FLAKY SEA SALT,
SUCH AS JACOBSEN OR MALDON

SPECIAL EQUIPMENT

CANDY THERMOMETER

Preheat the oven to 250°F. Line a baking sheet with parchment.

Butter a very large bowl. Pour in the popped popcorn.

In a medium heavy saucepan, combine the brown sugar, corn syrup, 2 tablespoons water, the butter, and fine sea salt and give it all a good stir, then cook over medium heat, stirring, until the sugar has dissolved and the butter is completely melted. Insert a candy thermometer and cook until the mixture reaches 250°F, about 5 minutes.

Remove the pan from the heat and quickly but carefully whisk in the vanilla and baking soda. The mixture

will bubble and foam and start to lighten in color.

Pour all of the caramel goo over the popcorn, using a heatproof spatula to make sure that it is all coated as evenly as possible. Stir in the almonds.

Spread the caramelized popcorn on the prepared baking sheet in a single layer. Bake for 45 minutes to 1 hour, tossing it every 15 minutes or so and checking for color toward the end of baking, until the popcorn is golden brown and smells delicious. Sprinkle with the flaky sea salt. Set aside to cool completely or eat it warm!

The popcorn can be stored at room temperature in an airtight container for up to 3 days.

SORGHUM-MOLASSES CHIPS

MAKES ½ POUND

These are one of my absolute favorite candies. They are based on the classic honeycomb candy, except we use sorghum molasses instead. Sorghum has a slightly sweet earthy flavor, which adds a deep richness to this candy that is pretty amazing.

1½ CUPS SUGAR

3 TABLESPOONS UNSALTED BUTTER

¼ TEASPOON CREAM OF TARTAR

½ CUP SORGHUM MOLASSES
(SEE PAGE 102)

2½ TEASPOONS BAKING SODA

6 OUNCES DARK COATING CHOCOLATE

SPECIAL EQUIPMENT

CANDY THERMOMETER

Line a baking sheet with parchment.

In a large heavy saucepan, combine the sugar, ⅓ cup water, the butter, and the cream of tartar and heat over medium heat, stirring to dissolve the sugar. Insert a candy thermometer and bring the mixture to a boil, without stirring, then cook until it registers 250°F.

Add the molasses, without stirring, and continue to boil until the sugar mixture registers 295°F. Remove from the heat, sift the baking soda over the mixture, and whisk for 10 to 20 seconds to incorporate. The mixture will bubble up—don't be alarmed, that will create the honeycomb texture.

Quickly pour the candy onto the prepared baking sheet (do not spread the mixture) and let cool completely. Once the candy has cooled, break it into pieces about 2 inches in size.

continued

Put the chocolate in a heatproof bowl, set the bowl over a saucepan of simmering water (make sure the bottom of the bowl doesn't touch the water), and melt the chocolate, stirring occasionally, until smooth. Remove from the heat.

Using tongs or a fork, dip each piece of candy into the chocolate to coat it fully, then shake the excess chocolate from it and place on the prepared baking sheet. Let the chocolate cool and set.

Store the chips in an airtight container at room temperature for up to 1 month.

SORGHUM IS LIQUID GOLD

Sorghum is one of my favorite ingredients. Its flavor is very complex: rich, sweet, fruity, caramely, and a little earthy, all at the same time. Sorghum is often used in biscuits, pies, and cakes, but you can also add a little to soups, sauces, and vinaigrettes. It is like liquid gold in our kitchen because it gives such character to everything it touches.

Sorghum syrup is a Southern ingredient that dates back to the mid-1800s. Traditionally sorghum production was a family-centered business, and even today it is still made by a few families who honor the history and old-world methods of milling sorghum by horse or mule, crushing the stalks, and then cooking the syrup in large vats over an open fire.

Although it is often referred to as sorghum molasses because it is thick, golden, and rich, sorghum is not molasses at all. It is made from the stalks of sweet sorghum cane, while molasses is a by-product of refined sugar.

RESOURCES

We have included in this list some of our absolute favorite places in Savannah and online. If you visit any of our local Savannah shops, be sure to tell them that we sent you!

Anson Mills
(803) 467-4122
ansonmills.com

An artisanal mill in South Carolina that hand-mills grits, rice, cornmeal, and specialty flours from organic heirloom grains.

Anthropologie
(800) 309-2500
anthropologie.com

I love their vintage-inspired home goods like the copper measuring cups, beautiful hand-painted measuring spoons, bakeware, and whisks.

Bell'occhio
10 Brady Street
San Francisco, CA 94103
(415) 864-4048
bellocchio.com

A wonderland filled with treasures and charm. I love to use the blackboard oilcloth to write my menu displays and the filet mignon string bag to take to the farmers' market. Bonus—all purchases are gift-wrapped in their signature snappy wrapping.

Emily Isabella
(608) 695-8846
emilyisabella.com

We love Emily's note cards and tea towels—especially the one inspired by her favorite bakers.

Etsy
etsy.com

An online community of artisans buying and selling handcrafted and vintage items.

Everyday Is a Holiday
everyday-is-a-holiday.blogspot .com

Art inspired by baked goods and vintage treasures? Yes, please! We adore our sign from them, which says, "Keep calm and have a cupcake."

Fabrika
**2 East Liberty Street
Savannah, GA 31401
fabrikafinefabrics.com**

Fabrics, notions, and gifts.

Fishs Eddy
**889 Broadway
New York, NY 10003
(212) 420-9020
fishseddy.com**

Vintage dishes, glasses, and serveware, kitchen linens, and so much more. It's a treasure trove of everything I love all in one place.

Hedley & Bennett
**(213) 744-1355
hedleyandbennett.com**

Our absolute favorite source for cooking aprons. They are made in the U.S.A., and they are good-looking too. We wear them loud and proud.

Herriott Grace
**(647) 340-5040
herriottgrace.com**

A supplier of hand-carved and hand-turned wooden objects, including rolling pins, cake pedestals, spoons, and serving boards, as well as kitchen linens, cake flags, and cookie cutters.

Jacobsen Salt Co.
**(503) 719-4973
jacobsensalt.com**

Beyond their flake and kosher sea salts, this nationally recognized brand also offers a wide variety of seasonings, spice blends, and other pantry staples.

Katie Runnels
(479) 684-6885
theconstantgatherer.com

Vintage treasures, including my collection of cupcake toppers. Katie, a mixed-media artist, says she is inspired by her love of family traditions, vintage wares, and Cheryl's buttercream frosting.

King Arthur Flour
(800) 827-6836
kingarthurflour.com

An employee-owned company that has been making pure flours (including almond flour) for more than two hundred years and is an essential source for baking supplies.

Layer Cake Shop
layercakeshop.com

A one-stop shop for adding vintage charm to homemade cupcakes and other treats. You will find powdered food coloring, luster dust, colored sanding sugar, and many other things to allow you to be creative in the kitchen.

Nordic Ware
(877) 466-7342
nordicware.com

Known for creating the Bundt pan, this family-owned business produces quality bakeware and kitchen tools that will become family heirlooms.

Oh Happy Day
shop.ohhappyday.com

Oh, let the party begin. This is my favorite one-stop shop for all things festive and fun. Looking for cake toppers, favors and gifts, tabletop accessories, or confetti balloons? You will find it all right here.

The Paris Market & Brocante
36 West Broughton Street
Savannah, GA 31401
(912) 232-1500
theparismarket.com

Located in the heart of Savannah's historic district, the Paris Market is a beautiful storehouse of treasures, filled with visual eye candy.

Prospector Co.

prospectorco.com

This online shop carries many of my favorite things, from kitchen soaps to candles to home decor.

Scharffen Berger

(855) 972-0511
shop.scharffenberger.com

This artisanal manufacturer offers a large selection of balanced and complex chocolates made from the finest cacao.

Shop Sweet Lulu

702 Center Road
Frankfort, IL 60423
(815) 464-6264
shopsweetlulu.com

Lovely food packaging and party-styling essentials sourced from all over the world.

Sucre Shop

sucreshop.com

The colorful hand-printed wooden utensils and plates are not only eco-friendly but also just the perfect touch for setting the table for a dinner party or holiday celebration.

Tiny Things Are Cute

tinythingsarecute.com

You'll find many tiny things here, such as cupcake flags, vintage gumball trinkets, and party favors.

West Elm

(888) 922-4119
westelm.com

A great source for cooks' tools and bakeware. We especially love their collaborations with handcraftspeople from all over the world.

INDEX

CONVERSION CHARTS

Here are rounded-off equivalents between the metric system and the traditional systems that are used in the United States to measure weight and volume.

FRACTIONS	DECIMALS
⅛	.125
¼	.25
⅓	.33
⅜	.375
½	.5
⅝	.625
⅔	.67
¾	.75
⅞	.875

WEIGHTS

US/UK	METRIC
¼ oz	7 g
½ oz	15 g
1 oz	30 g
2 oz	55 g
3 oz	85 g
4 oz	110 g
5 oz	140 g
6 oz	170 g
7 oz	200 g
8 oz (½ lb)	225 g
9 oz	250 g
10 oz	280 g
11 oz	310 g
12 oz	340 g
13 oz	370 g
14 oz	400 g
15 oz	425 g
16 oz (1 lb)	455 g

VOLUME

AMERICAN	IMPERIAL	METRIC
¼ tsp		1.25 ml
½ tsp		2.5 ml
1 tsp		5 ml
½ Tbsp (1½ tsp)		7.5 ml
1 Tbsp (3 tsp)		15 ml
¼ cup (4 Tbsp)	2 fl oz	60 ml
⅓ cup (5 Tbsp)	2½ fl oz	75 ml
½ cup (8 Tbsp)	4 fl oz	125 ml
⅔ cup (10 Tbsp)	5 fl oz	150 ml
¾ cup (12 Tbsp)	6 fl oz	175 ml
1 cup (16 Tbsp)	8 fl oz	250 ml
1¼ cups	10 fl oz	300 ml
1½ cups	12 fl oz	350 ml
2 cups (1 pint)	16 fl oz	500 ml
2½ cups	20 fl oz (1 pint)	625 ml
5 cups	40 fl oz (1 qt)	1.25 l

OVEN TEMPERATURES

	°F	°C	GAS MARK
very cool	250–275	130–140	½–1
cool	300	148	2
warm	325	163	3
moderate	350	177	4
moderately hot	375–400	190–204	5–6
hot	425	218	7
very hot	450–475	232–245	8–9

°C/F TO °F/C CONVERSION CHART

°C/F	°C	°F	°C/F	°C	°F	°C/F	°C	°F	°C/F	°C	°F
90	32	194	220	104	428	350	177	662	480	249	896
100	38	212	230	110	446	360	182	680	490	254	914
110	43	230	240	116	464	370	188	698	500	260	932
120	49	248	250	121	482	380	193	716	510	266	950
130	54	266	260	127	500	390	199	734	520	271	968
140	60	284	270	132	519	400	204	752	530	277	986
150	66	302	280	138	536	410	210	770	540	282	1,004
160	71	320	290	143	554	420	216	788	550	288	1,022
170	77	338	300	149	572	430	221	806			
180	82	356	310	154	590	440	227	824			
190	88	374	320	160	608	450	232	842			
200	93	392	330	166	626	460	238	860			
210	99	410	340	171	644	470	243	878			

Example: If your temperature is 90°F, your conversion is 32°C; if your temperature is 90°C, your conversion is 194°F.

Library of Congress Cataloging-in-Publication Data is on file.

Names: Day, Cheryl, author. | Day, Griffith, author.
Title: The Artisanal kitchen. Sweets and treats / Cheryl Day and Griffith Day.
Description: New York : Artisan, a division of Workman Publishing Co. Inc. [2018] |
    Includes an index.
Identifiers: LCCN 2018003630 | ISBN 9781579658601 (hardcover : alk. paper)
Subjects: LCSH: Brownies (Cooking) | Cupcakes. | Candy. | LCGFT: Cookbooks.
Classification: LCC TX771 .D39 2018 | DDC 641.86/53—dc23
LC record available at https://lccn.loc.gov/2018003630

Design by Erica Heitman-Ford

Artisan books are available at special discounts when purchased in bulk for premiums and sales promotions as well as for fund-raising or educational use. Special editions or book excerpts also can be created to specification. For details, contact the Special Sales Director at the address below, or send an e-mail to specialmarkets@workman.com.

For speaking engagements, contact speakersbureau@workman.com.

Published by Artisan
A division of Workman Publishing Co., Inc.
225 Varick Street
New York, NY 10014-4381
artisanbooks.com

Artisan is a registered trademark of Workman Publishing Co., Inc.

This book has been adapted from *The Back in the Day Bakery Cookbook* (Artisan, 2012) and *Back in the Day Bakery Made with Love* (Artisan, 2015).

Published simultaneously in Canada by Thomas Allen & Son, Limited

Printed in China
First printing, July 2018

10 9 8 7 6 5 4 3 2 1